T0294635

SONGS FOR TWO VOICES

PHOENIX **POETS**

BRUCE SMITH

Songs *for* Two Voices

THE UNIVERSITY OF CHICAGO PRESS
Chicago and London

BRUCE SMITH is professor of creative writing at Syracuse
University. His four books of poems include, *The Other Lover,*
which was a finalist for both the Pulitzer Prize and the
National Book Award in 2001.

The University of Chicago Press, Chicago 60637
The University of Chicago Press, Ltd., London
© 2005 by The University of Chicago
All rights reserved. Published 2005
Printed in the United States of America
14 13 12 11 10 09 08 07 06 05   1 2 3 4 5

ISBN: 0–226–76455–9 (cloth)

Library of Congress Cataloging-in-Publication Data

Smith, Bruce, 1946–
  Songs for two voices / Bruce Smith.
    p. cm. — (Phoenix poets)
  ISBN 0-226-76455-9 (alk. paper)
  I. Title. II. Series.
  PS3569 .M512S66 2005
  811'.54—dc22
                              2004024639

∞ The paper used in this publication meets the minimum
requirements of the American National Standard for
Information Sciences—Permanence of Paper for Printed
Library Materials, ANSI z39.48–1992.

To the memory of Josephine Preston Smith (1925–2000)

from #512

The Soul's retaken moments—
When, Felon led along,
With shackles on the plumed feet,
And staples, in the Song . . .

Emily Dickinson

Contents

Acknowledgments

The author wishes to thank the editors of the following journals in which versions of these poems have appeared:

American Poetry Review: "Song with Trucks in the Distance," "Song with Alabama in Drag," "Strong Female Lead," "Song of Loss in the Form of a Cock Ring"
Boston Review: "Song with a Child's Pacifier in It," "Song Disowned"
The Diagram: "How I Came to Believe in the Soul" (as "Song of the Soulist")
Fence: "Song of the Little Zion Baptist Church"
Greensboro Review: "Stills"
Gulf Coast: "Song of the Bad Infinite"
Harvard Review: "Song for My Daughter" (as "Letter to My Daughter in the Form of a Song of Person and Time")
Hunger Mountain: "Song of the Soul as Miles Davis"
Luna: "Double Portrait"
Paris Review: "Song of Sun Ra" (as "Song of Le Sony'r Ra")
Pool: "Song of the Ransom of the Dark"
Salt Hill: "Song of the Mother in the Snow," "Song with Cement," "Baby Needs a New Pair of Shoes" (as "Song of the Brogues Better than Letter and Spirit")
Washington Square: "Song After the Wedding After the War"
West Branch: "Song of the Least Thing"
Western Humanities Review: "Song with Spanish Shoes"
Windsor Review: "Reverse Cowgirl"

*   *   *

"Song with a Child's Pacifier in It" appeared in *The Best American Poetry Anthology, 2003,* edited by Yusef Komunyakaa.

"Song of the Ransom of the Dark" appeared in *The Best American Poetry Anthology, 2004,* edited by Lynn Hejenian.

"Song of the Little Zion Baptist Church" appeared in *The Pushcart Prize XXVI-II, Best of the Small Presses, 2004.*

A debt of immense and endless gratitude to Peter Balakian, Robin Behn, Chard deNiord, Jack Wheatcroft, Michael Burkhard, and Brooks Haxton.

SONGS FOR TWO VOICES

Song of the Least Thing

Because the father was small
buying all his clothes at Sears Fashions for Boys

the stylish non-style of mimed men's wear
their shoes and spoons and prayers were small

their Christs were small, their Yawehs infinitesimal
themselves slave to wage or the rain that falls in movies

the world soul could fit like a ham
on a platter or in a sock or trousers or skirt

Some Eros, some appetite was behind it
and there the world ended: the variety of garments

of Philadelphia, the flannels of work, the satins of dance
the khaki or Hi-Boy collars and pimped out pants

like the exercises of Ignatius: to see the black/white world
in its distinction before they saw majesty

how the radiant faces look down
They got sick looking into the grid of graph paper

on which in the kitchen they played Battleship
hit but not sunk, their destroyers

hid their subs amoebic, piddling
the light blue squares attached to one another

and lettered and numbered in a War
like the distant atom-split, Japanese neutron

Why not a new science for each distinct thing
The faucet's drip into the ocean

their American, unreal, poverty, a cyclonic wind
Some Eros, some appetite behind it

In this place they became realists of the meager
motives twisted in the shoelaces of the kid

*   *   *

I surrender my selves to you as a small boy
before the school yard bully of the snake brain

made to survive the fire, the fang, the insult
before learning to chew or play the piano, sacrificing

selves to know summer, winter, the meanwhile
no sense of time line, story boards

of socialization. I adore you
means muster the long black ships

rage is a measure of beauty
I own the angry, camouflage and dazzle

I split into alibi and Buddha-boy
I adore you

means have my pathology call your pathology
your mother—blowsy, beautiful, derelict

and dear old dad—taciturn, tender, feckless
I surrender to the bully of beauty you are

I surrender to the narcotics
of dopamine and serontin

to déjà vu and the necessary coo to
the ego, home movies of Narcissus and wish

I surrender the knife and the lamp
I surrender to the rust-belt city of salt and snow

No rationing, honey, *all* not *some*
Repetition, provocation, compulsion, crying

I surrender. I've forgotten, like the Israelites,
who I was and where and what god. I adore you

as the one through whom I became unhappy
fearful of the pleasure I surrender to

Song of the Pronouns

Propped up with pillows, my mother was the queen
of ice cream—the only thing besides the morphine

she asked for, being all diva
all nitrogen in its cycle, all amen

all women who have served and stood at attention
a century shrunk to a mouth swabbed by sponges

after months of hospice where she girled
and babied and animaled and single-celled

and was a face of all nada
our breathing, our parsing, our oohs and ahs

as we dressed and undressed her in costumes
as she darkened into Aida with no tongue

slave to what unbecomes
We gathered the family just she and us

she blurred our faces, scrapings
of the brain pan like the ice cream's last spoonings

nameless bits of gristle grit
of her teeth and swoon and eye roll as she said

Oh, this one (my brother) *and this one* (the prodigal
son she called me) she sings to no one

we know *Oh*
I've got plenty of nothing

                    *   *   *

       Elegy after the elegy—*Will she stop dying
       please?* I thought I was finished with her

       the lapse and sadness and keen days
       in which all cripplings were suspended

       all unjust taxings, *no mas,* all further martyrdoms amended
       by mothers and all sunderings hammered together by men

       good for something finally, for their steel and repetition
       compulsion. In the regime which resembled a bland, unsnarled

       version of the bygone—the rhapsody and gnarled
       life we called living by rubbing the faces off coins

       I did this; I did that, like Frank O'Hara
       and who was more vulgar and fine in his mascara

       than me with my corrective shoes and bag of medicines
       and my eggbeater for solidarity with dada and fictions

       made for love? In the glorious, in the glamorous
       survival under the sunsets, under the snow

which uses everything like a bankrupt culture
forced to make do with the leavings

in this administration of affection
(or not) fails the little life of Blackie White Paws

unaccountable piece of spittle, licked fur
and hissing domestic misdemeanor that unravels

the whole system—its sentences and pronouncements and gavel
bangings that cancel the contract we once had between

pronouns and nouns, between the seen and the unseen
between our world trembling

and our not unkind dissembling
and this is my elegy

Song of the Mother in the Snow

Her voice crossed with the reports
of January weather, two degrees

muffled by snow, cold rubbing
against the warm, molecular frictions

in a dreamwork
that makes distance, *right here,* she says

*I'm right here. It's just a little touch
of the cancer. I can't talk anymore*

She thinks a phone call was a wired
bewilderment of great expense

and she an operator
a dit-dat artist, a lightning slinger

in fake nylons and lipstick
imagining a soldier calling home

She keeps it short, the details of the chemicals
but not the pain as if that is something

that falls and drifts and vanishes
and then the mouth vanishes

*   *   *

The *I* is the echo, the little bang, the buzz
a broadcast beginning with the rumor

then a spindle of sugar and acid held
by a hydrogen bond, an illusion of a life in the skin

then being the issue and edit of the human
the lovely technicality of someone *and*

demon, the violent internal conversation
felon of self and others I take for

myself at great expense and distance
connected to the source

substituting the voice for the body
echoed, the copied and manifold is real

if brief, the switch and shunt of electrons
isn't that I: the vexed, the contested life

huge insinuations and the mere
interference, wires twined

Song of Sun Ra

I came to Alabama for the dreams
impossible, uninhabitable bottom land and unreconstructed

self, you must not say every manner of redneck
and Negroes you must not say and red clay Diaspora

sons and daughters of cherubim and Cherokee, townies
county workers, the displaced academics and those that would be

elsewhere in the correctional facility, you must not say slammer
or Paris. I came for the poverty. Hadn't I lost everything

in Cambridge and New York, in Providence? A fly trapped inside
with as much body I remain and this is a dream

I came for the apparel of the NuSouth, which I found
in a South Carolina haberdashery run by two brothers

(I came for brotherhood) who sell the threads that bind us
for the sons of former slaves and the sons of former slave owners

But what if I am daughter? It makes me anyway cry
I came for the tears, the trail. I came for the intersections

of Bear Bryant and Martin Luther King and Lurleen Wallace
the trivia of everywhere and everyone from somewhere

as some form of race baiter, race traitor, scat back
and Gandhi. Aren't we just suffragettes

in T-shirts? Aren't we bantamweight, failed populists
retreating to the history of one? Didn't we bring the five-string

to meet the devil in the Black Belt? I came for the football
the male drag and the dragons—the race drag

and the pulled pork—the drag of homicidal human life
and class war. I came to be projected back

(a reclamation project): to the CORE volunteers
and to eat Kings' last meal of catfish and hushpuppies

with the feeling of indignity and righteousness
I came for the slowing, the bend in the Black Warrior River

where the essence could change, but slowly, like an age
Triassic, 35 million years of gymnosperm and insect

translated as maidenhair, ginkgo, loblolly pine and cockroach
I came for the sorority and fraternity

that would not have me as a member. I came
who else would have me? for the states rights

and color codes and Freedom Riders singing
to walk where they walked it would be my sacrifice

and vision and my privilege this is a dream
to be the stop along the underground railroad

of the blood. And the train goes by in Tuscaloosa
and it's all we know of human longing

This is a dream. I came for dreams
I came to be someone's property. I came to be

fifty and without property, three-fifths a man
two-fifths a woman, you must not say this is you

*   *   *

Of Sun Ra, who said he was born on another
planet, but was a blue baby of Birmingham, Alabama

an archangel of Egypt or Saturn if you were blood
in the 30s , what is there to say

Music is the alter-place, slices of standards
freakouts, Latin dance, chants, calls for

all demons, Caribbean or other. Home was telescoped
Ethiope: he can be from anywhere he chooses

the world an orphans' home like Bishop's
in Brazil, or magnified grainy landscapes

of Dixie: the blackface anthem for a land
of cotton, played at the inauguration

of Jefferson Davis, in Montgomery, Alabama
the impossible attracts me, because everything possible

has been done and the world didn't change
impossible the watchword of the great space age

of angels of which he is one, he said, and Coleman Hawkins
and Fletcher Henderson, are ones of a culture and beauty

astral, necessary, alien, not born but arrived
from another planet, shape-shifted from history

to mystery, my story, he said
like Baptists or Muslims, the unconverted are dead

Flying or walking the narrow path
of the spirituals, the conversion myths

of jazz, whatever that is, and the black name
and the spirit being put on the robes of utopia

John Brown's heavenly march
to the science fiction film we live in now

and in the future: his music
an answer to the place

of the stars beyond where he lived
Chicago in the 50s, New York in 1960

with *wings unhampered/unafraid . . . /soaring*
in outer space as inner space

a collective improvisation on a large scale
to save the planet

you thought it was just for the art
Counter, as in the ring shouts, stomped out

sorrow, stomped out all the red clay
when in a fracas with the cops

a voice said *leave the motherfucker
alone,* and he did not know

that the Creator spoke in such a tongue
struck dumb, hearing voices, sudden transportation

renamed Ra, son of the trickster gods
from the poor, obscure pianist from Alabama

Song of Loss in the Form of a Cock Ring

In order to say what cannot be said
In order to speak the word, *loss*

put the tip of your tongue against the top front teeth
lightly, the tongue sorrowed in its spit

the lips in a flattened O as the teeth close
almost, the breath released through the slit

loss. I know you find it cruel
in the likenesses of the word to *gloss*

to *lust* to *lash*
to *less and less* to *ash*

that tragic 5 Act. It is cruel in the complicity
of skin and rain. We met. The room dim

jet fuel smell, smuggled fruit, the curtain
of I am and am I? blown open

the coil and uncoil of the dawn, that black out/lights up
cruel as a barbed wire bracelet

I wore until it *X*ed me into
one of my names, the others being

I can say now: The Syllable, The Bundle, The Shuck and Jive
the Tangle, the Torso where the fluids were kept

Your name was different in each version of
the story that engine that heart that *X*

the anonymous, the treasure, the cross out, the exposition
that fails you on the edge of route six somewhere

between the romance and the seized cylinder
your face in the headlights wanting metaphysics

holding your breath until you came

              *   *   *

        The song I was listening to rhymed
        devotion and *emotion,* binding

        together the ache, the fruit, the fruit picking
        the picked fruit and those that picked the fruit

        for us while we bite into the fur of the peach
        the sensible ravishment of *hunger* and *sugar*

        and *warmonger,* where for a taste
        of the fondant we stole—like Augustine

        like Teddy Roosevelt in the Latin America
        With devotion comes someone's

bully pulpit and eye rhyme
body over body, claimed by a voice

I was thinking of someone else
you were thinking of your father's limbs

god in his basketball shorts
I was thinking of Sarah Vaughan

her song, "Body and Soul"
I was your father, his story

You were the darker version
of her. Forget the *bereft/theft* rhyme

It was a gift to remember
you: all the talk and the body uncoiled

and coiled, the purple—suffering the pleasures
the grip at the base, the noose like a leash

outside the jets, the morning a peach
It was a gift, I mean, you were a gift

Song with Alabama in Drag

As if the state were expressing, *X* pressing
what was lost—the war, the way

the waiting to have and to be
so she puts on clothes: berry-colored shift

the color of crepe myrtle and a velvet pillbox hat
with a chocolate crocodile handbag, matching shoes

heels like needles. Her hair permed: This
is a woman, whatever that is. She comes out

of the closet, but into what? The red clay
of skinned infields, green diamonds, and the brilliant

gridirons lit as if by flares and marked and sprinkled
like a Baptist sect: so in September

she may put on the girdle and the shoulder pads
and strut, stutter step, juke, and bull rush

in order to find the crease and glorify the end zone
and point to god-as-humid-night, the night beyond loss

to the black belt cinched with cotton and catfish
farms: the blunt and flooded, revisionist diamonds

of mud and trailer court. She's sad
in her blush, her berry brulée lipstick, walking

the boulevards of camellia and Coach Bryant
the intersections of drama and plasma, skin

and mime, butch and femme, walking
home, whatever that is: the church

of engine strut and gown in the pawn shop window
the Ionic columns, land expressed into lawn where

in the dusk the sprinklers come out to recite
the past, the past, the past, the past, the past

　　　　　*　　　　　*　　　　　*

　　　　Whatever skin I'm in
　　　　whatever it is I will die doing

　　　　writing, loving Marlene
　　　　again, my head in her lap

　　　　for the photograph, an image of John the Baptist
　　　　what a man wants: his head in the middle of a woman

　　　　and a sentiment, like the recognition of parting
　　　　that comes with the first button undone, something

　　　　sorrowed inside her, her hair raked with fingers
　　　　temporary loss of time and pronouns

doomed to be uncoupled, to be obvious
or hidden. Don't forget that part

lying here in my blue pajamas bottoms
reflected in a smoky mirror, low-level event

I remember the actress with MS
who wants to be a name on Broadway or off

a bit part, gratifying the self that survives
though the body, whatever that is, dies acting

Acting: the time between call back and out of work
we love you but

Song with a Child's Pacifier in It

Indolent days in exile from Alabama in a city
in the north I was bussed into: *I don't hate it*

I don't hate it I don't, where the streets around the sublet
are cordoned off for excavating water mains

and electrical cables strung from the Transcendentalists
When the hot-patch truck backs up it makes the sound

of an ambulance in France and the air is perfumed
with the lacquered black oil spilled

at a great distance from Arabia and Pec, then mopped up
and tamped in a form of a coffin. A fine film over the new

a planetary dust. In the gutter an imitation pearl
plastic tiara, a winged copy of *Spare Change*

an oven mitt, a child's pacifier
a lipstick casing, a pencil

but who would write except the indolent? Hidden
speakers transmit the songs of

Cubanismo who will play a benefit for *la causa*
ritmo. It's all in the rib cage, the salsa

A partially repatriated émigré with a crushed hat, I carry
in a wheelbarrow my heterosexual agenda

difference (and shame and shamelessness)
I return to the smoke of time

in Boston when I loved the numinous
and now I await the dream trials

where exhibit A is rhythm, exhibit B a curl of hair
wrapped around a finger then unwound stretched

from the Balkans through policy through rapture of the past
to Tuscaloosa where I will delay the verdict with a song

        *   *   *

       Philadelphia was a school
       of cinderblocks and John Wayne, I do

       black like a white kid in detention
       erotic possibilities of wrongness like a guitar

       I plucked, all adrenaline and vibration
       b-twang squeak, a language

       of hurt in sweet, predestined ways
       and volition like a little philosopher of hell

       I argued to myself, said scat and blasphemous prayers
       The city was another world inside this one

glaze over the beads of the glorified
an oven, an ocean passage, a lost nation

Can you remember this? Akhmatova was asked
I remember the air in summer was an atom flow

karmic missiles, marines and a boy
It's all in the belly button, the coach says

the outside boy of body, the inside boy of mind
that schizophrenia I will carry to the flame and ash

In the city I fell in love with Mistress Errato
and the difference and the evening light

For the crimes of 1965, your honor
I'm sorry. I accuse myself of wanting a life

willful and fatal, enraged and tender, the lifelong split
of the self: in the American tar and becoming uneasy

Song with Trucks in the Distance

You do yet taste
Some subtleties of the isle, that will not let you
Believe things certain

—THE TEMPEST

Summer was a radio thrown in the bath

  The voices of the dead speaking, but far away, of things betrayed

Summer sounded, sounded like, distance

  like the big rigs on the interstate, running tonnage or empty

Summer was the sensation rushed

  between engulfed and abandoned, the two wishes

Summer bottled like a jinn, and the flags of the sweet pea

  ruby and white, saturated so that they weep light

Summer was the soul of a girl who swims

  the two rivers of becoming and evening

in summer, in the public pool, and becomes what drowns her

  Can I ransom the time? Hurt her back into being

summer to heal you have to hurt first

five iambs on the rib cage and breathe

into summer as into hunger for the butter

into the form, her lips glistened I remember

summer: gold threaded, dyer's rocket, sulfur, the Yellow Pages

Can I redeem the walls for upholding her shoulders

Summer was pure fuckery

and my hands for that percussion stopped in the middle of

Summer: the rain delay, the curfew, the dallying

that porch sitting or corpse washing or

Summer the singularity or the classless stars falling

weather, whatever you want to call it. I called it

Summer, a thought can lift the body politic

away: carried, called, stolen

Summer was the outpatient psychiatric unit

alien, fugitive, volatile as oils, hopeless as if

Summer channeled Marcus Garvey and the Quaker martyrs

being a girl in America is being the changeling

Summer channeled Dallas and Damascus

of time I will have to repay in other time

Summer was the taste of her menstrual blood, the death of us

in other ways and winds: the papaguyo through the windows

of summer of blacktop, summer of world-ash, summer of shadow

of Somerville, the mistral and cloud towers of New York

Summer was suffering the sea-change in the hydrant spray

and the blackthorn winters of the boroughs

Summer, advancing issues lead declines

My debt is for the perfume and the aliases

Summer was M. Moth Wing, Mme. Alabama

I assumed in the Florentine shadows. It was

Summer we Platoed our ways

as European as I've ever been. Thank you for that

Summer who betrayed whom? I missed that part of the movie

Time was borrowed and compounded, time was

Summer a towel thrown over the animal

a lost hound, time muttered yeah, yeah, yeah

Summer everyone was drinking something called "Soul"

How can I repay her for the girl slang

Summer blade of grass between our thumbs

and the blossom of paper, the gun in the river

Summer, four years from when I left

the bullets on the table by the bed

Song of the Afterlife

In the afterlife the lines were too long
I wanted (in the afterlife and I still *wanted!*)

to meet Dostoyevski (who spoke no English)
and Dickinson (who spoke no word)

Long lines to sit opposite Blake
and sip bad coffee of the afterlife

so I talked to the man beside me
whom I met in New York in 1974, now dead

of the HIV, who told me that he lived
for poetry, he said this walking east on 8th Street

under a street light in a cold wind. He said
poetry failed him and fluid filled his lungs

and here he was in line to meet Donne
or was this the Ovid line? Where was this going

I asked a woman who looked like someone
tired from eight hours on her feet, eight years

on her feet, serving, someone I loved once
She said, with you it is always thinking

as a form of desire, of wanting, like sexual wanting
that loss of tongue, that undoing, the beauty of others

coveted. Ha, she said, with you
its always sentiment. Go fuck yourself

with your letters, your laments. Sniffing
after greatness. Your love and death

What time is it? she said
I said, This is the afterlife. We have no time

That's what you think she said
turning away. Desire keeps you dying

Go on and live in your little oblivion.

      *   *   *

    In this life he failed
    in Philadelphia in his appeal to the Powers

        that Be and the Dominions that would send him first
        to Fort Dix, New Jersey among those

        dog faces, bullet baits, zipperheads, bullshit
        artists, his people who were conscripted

        long lines, bad chow, he gagged from the gas
        and his epiphanies were deferred. He feared death

        experienced as desire which led to groveling
        sympathies with a vengeful god

three-personed: the god of the erection
the god of mutability

the masochistic god of success
Where was I

he said when he landed in Vietnam
He wanted to submit to the monster-mistress

from his own rib and bound to him
bliss or woe spending his marrow

in his/her arms when he should be
war mongering or being

for a minute inside her or him
succubae that drew from the groin through the spine

That explains the depression, Aristotle
said, after intercourse

self-squandered, death-kissed
letters he sent home had no

name, rank, serial number
In this life he foreclosed on what he saw

that other self who did his duty
to be beloved by his country

by giving himself up in tiny little pieces

Song of the Bad Infinite

I'm in Boston with the self-renewing liver
and the insatiable vulture, while my friend's

in Iowa on the train through Des Moines
to Omaha, going West, a daytime wrestle

with the Angel of the manifest.
He's lost in the corn, in the tasselling wind.

In Boston I'm giving up, giving in, giving down, strange
charm and bottom: the flavors of quarks in which I taste

myself, my satisfied thirst for the unsatisfied
the partial, the self sweaty and empty and filled

with the whole, the amplitudes and frequencies of
mis hermanos y mis hermanas

whose vehicle is heat shimmer and spray
from the sprinkler, whose medium is Kool Aid

and government cheese. The least love
I had was the Mass General Outpatient

Psychiatric Clinic where I signed for the other
when she slit her wrists on the Platonic

perfume bottle in an August like this
I found how useless the passion was

how useless the god was. I told my friend I was hot
but happy to be in the apartheid of Boston

where I could spend hours in the dark
of The Brattle Theater dilated, watching the noir

holding the darkness as a bride
and hugging it in mine arms

*   *   *

Summer of the sucker MCs and hip-hop music
black blood filter and fiber like Whitman with a mic

stupid rope gold, playing the dozens
getting paid, whatever rhymes

with money. Sampled bass and sax
clean extended remix, scratch and break

with the old, old music of tambour and oud
skins and a tin can and an empty bottle

Naming confers meaning and cash
shake what you've got, sez the soul in paraphrase

ten years ago. Does *ago* always mean *naive*?
Ten years before, Wild Style, on the pearly linoleum

laid out for the dance, The Freeze, the notched occasion
forms of renaming and adorning the soul

gumbo of pleasure and power
in the house means business and presence

and stank, a terrible presence, a negative miracle
of the body and the simultaneous

joy and lamentation of women
ten years of gettin' paid, and *on and on*

till the break of dawn
I can't stop and I won't stop

Baby Needs a New Pair of Shoes

More than my nation I miss my shoes
as I marched toward the horizon

that looked like the Kazak on the floor
of my home: hereafter every time we say *home*

we must add *so to speak* to indicate it is a syllable
a sigh and expression that stretches from the trellis

white with clematis to the men in a tank
at the border. Hereafter a pair of shoes

will ransom my nation. Between the Romeo slippers
I wear (like a *pasha,* my wife says)

at home (*so to speak*) and the Italian calf-skin
wedding and funeral shoes

I wear the everyday brogues that just yesterday
I had resoled by Haxhi and propped up at the café

My children march (homeless) so to speak
they are a team of America in their sneakers

a defeated team with no hoops or cheers
A ball is the ransom of my nation

There is no time for the heat
of the mind or its equivalents, the lovely shell

the sun turns into and the evening asleep
in its clothes by the side of the road

where there's a poppy, a woman's hair clip
an empty cartridge from a weapon

I had the fevered feeling of return
as I almost slept. Mind be buried in body

be hidden in feet in these shoes, the tanned hide
the welt and seam, the counter and quarter

the tongue where death can't find me

       *   *   *

Baby needs a new pair of shoes
the wish on the discarded cards

shunt and jumble, crank and draw, then the dole
and the rewish for three of something, a full house

counting the cards but losing track, reading
the faces, loving the slang: Hollywood (acting)

or leather (patience), it's the most
we will have of solidarity

as criminal and buddy and thrilled
in the bind and the spill and the loss

not loss. We gave money to each other
We loved the charity and thin dominion

We owed and itched, kibitzed, the talk
not talk, the excess beyond necessity

Tonic and smoke and the cold meats
It's already tomorrow, someone would say to a pair

of two fat ladies in the smoke I listened for my name
as we tore apart the spread

and muttered the coded, countervailing word
flop and bump you, flicker and beggar, hands

of rockets, monsters, immortals, a packed house
or rags, a piece of cheese, a monkey flush, the utterance

the next AM when the sun is a camera flash
at the scene, traces of the kings' endless questions

a cigarette butt floats in the lukewarm beer
like a dash between letter and spirit, I—You

wandering in the unconjugated verbs, the further
wish, the incarnation of the bluff and luxury

the muck of the word disclosed
I see you and I raise you

Song of the Suffering of the Pencil

She copied out the face of Christ from a book of Brueghel

    While I watched the Yanks on TV

with the same scourged lord face

    with the fan's passionate distraction of one seized by

her face—animal elegy and beauty—to worship

    Caesar—lover of dominion, lover of the three-run homer

the observance of

    the high hard stuff, the redundancy

all orders to glory

    in ball two, the world proved frail

all the all

    So I loved Win Big, Win Ugly

Christ's face as if he were a Texan

throwing smoke, split-fingered, punching him out

Christ's a guy with secrets, bearing

being a collaborator with the powers

the cross of his work, his death

that be, so loathing that in me

so loathing that in him

the part of me that makes its monuments of wood

Through the suffering of the pencil

the Etruscan part that feels the weariness

we might see differently, the beauty

of the bat, the ash and willow, and the spectacle

the comeliness of the bruise, the wound

of the average fattened on fastballs

and the guy numbered with the transgressors

the humiliations of the circus, the dominant eye and hand

if she can get it down

of the batter. Worship the skill

if she can bring him back from his slaughter

  worship the criminal, worship the empire

we can be saved by what's becoming in her face

  power to all fields

Song for My Daughter

There is a space both small and vast between
your offspringing and your womaning that is my life

that has in it *Hunger Strikers*
those words you echoed from the evening news

and bread that I baked that was no answer
to the hunger, although it tasted good with butter

Your mother was Hans Holbein in the basement
I was Erasmus in the study. You, the child of artisans

of shadow and shortage, rode your Bat Cycle
through the vast corridors of the red brick dormitory

we lived in having fled rents and Reaganomics
for the ceremony of serving by standing, waiting

I was the lay minister and JV football coach
to the stars: Kennedys and mesomorphic debutantes

with temperatures to be taken, Jewish
Mandarin-speaking middle linebackers

L=A=N=G=U=A=G=E poets in training
You grew up in the late renaissance

and then it was over. Money had won
and the brothers multiplied in prisons

like black hermaphroditic rabbits
Time was stage fright—afraid we'd miscarry

the persons we were and all the etiquettes
that gave us an agitated space

in which to live would become the bad likeness of the time
that middle class lie that tasted good with butter

I strapped you in the car seat and drove to Boston
a small space to witness the scrimmage of memory and desire

like two Hindu deities vanishing or appearing
with a million brilliant eyes

I practiced my *sheer contemporary* and my *absolute present*
in a scarf and a work shirt on which your mother sewed a fritillary

when we loved each other and we did
in our house inside a school, a miniature, Socratic life

worrying as a form of longing
as the bread was rising

*   *   *

The odd old country of my father
patched, wool gathered, clocked in musical time

slow, *larghetto; calando,* gradually diminishing
he lived in the evening news—an island that exported terror

and nightmare where there is no art
where they do everything as well as they can

I did not know if he were dove or Strangelove in the basement
where he went for his darling

prisoner of what muffled and thrilled him
Rummaging I found a shoe box

with a single syllable and a photograph
of time as he knew it

hostile, bewitched, anticlimactic, miraculous
When he went dead

without telling his desire
his language was the ash of

failing to be the great god
of love, the great god of details

His song: *sforzato,* forced; *rubato,* robbed
of time and so freed from being a man

odd, a woman in the eyes of the world
What he was was a nervous realist

in a sentimental domain, a lover
not a fighter, and I was surprised

he knew the terms and would put them
with pencil on paper fixing me

when I would be moved by his flowing hand
Logos living and changing like the snake

that vacationed from school with us and died
in his closet in a shoe box

Song after the Wedding after the War

Paradise was acid, wanted leaf rot, bone meal, and time
the dirt was salty and the lake was a metal

we had no name for. There were wild strawberries
mealy fruit for no one. In paradise the seething

was peaceful and the wounding cordial
those sitting down to pastry and a coffee

would speak their hearts among the cups and saucers
that was poetry—speaking our three-chambered hearts

our four-fingered poems among chipped plates and spoons
our hearts trapped in the body of

others: the firmaments of the troubled milk
the fundaments of the perpetual fire . . .

In paradise we needed the fire to make the cake
and we needed the sacrifice to make the doctrine

and we needed the doctrine to make the dolce
for the gods who were stilled only by the stolen sweetness

or fullness and we had our fill and the graves were full
and it was not enough. She wanted more than she wanted

he wanted Want dead like the Buddha
or he wanted a Want baby

or Want breath with his name
on the lips of others. He wanted

fullness emptied and she wanted emptiness filled
They would agree on this: difference. Was this any way to be wed

So sadness came down on them like rain on a lake
and they emptied into each other and were filled

and it tasted like ash and salt: the looking back and the leaving
they spilled over and when it would end it would be

         *   *   *

      Wanted more than You/I, wanted many plots
      unsettled, various, large and extravagant as love

      in a Russian novel. Maybe medicinal, maybe forbidden
      cleaved as a cell is cleaved into cancer or cure or another

      swirly mist, the dark, prophetic weather
      you could slop something into and confess to

      the rut, the bounce, the bearing down of
      your lips, my lips, your urge, my stop

      me before I kill again, pronouns as answer and call
      alloys of the dreadful, the devoted, the metaphorical

Then one day in the fall, the end of metaphor
the apocalypse killed the running joke

a man with a sign saying EVERYTHING
WILL BE ALRIGHT (like a Bob Marley song)

the telling over. Over the light, the luxury
and still you wanted to wed

something with something
or nothing with nothing

mutual pleasure, mutual power
for the wedding they needed flowers

Was this even the time for flowers
The delphiniums with their dolphin shaped nectary

or mums with their gold heads redolent
of football. No more *like,* just then

Song of the Ransom of the Dark

A neural, feral fix on the beautiful movie face
like a baby bird imprinted to the worst affliction

havoc, holocaust, from my seat in the dark
while I sipped a Coke. A movie set, a rear projection

a lot of junk it seems, yet
it's where the conversation started

a back and forth like flame in wind
It is where love came from

as fetish—a wrist, a thigh, a foot in heels
all of what we wanted

fatality and church and commodity
something about to burst

into my lap from my purchase in
a plush paranoia of the glance

of horror or color in our *Wizard of Oz*
or *Apocalypse Now* or *Notorious*

hard to horrify, hard to please
I can't remember in the film why in the first place

the government hired Ingrid Bergman
but I remember the head lights and the curve

the fragment of music, the set of keys
like coins or slow rain

and a moment when the black white
faces are all there are

an infinitely prolonged walk up the stairways
dizzying and it's not the horror

but the pleasure that can be found daily
the infinitely prolonged kiss

encircling glances, tracking shots, arabesques
the one dialect of shadow and the war, the girl

the eye dilated

          *   *   *

      I went to Vietnam to adopt a kid
      I wanted meaning in my life

      Poetry had failed me
      slowly poetry had failed me

      first as grace, then as skin, then
      as woman—as the raveled end of all my being

      plucked up again and woven
      to purl and circle

you like the mats and baskets of this country
the squat huts the women carrying the rain

in silty baskets between the first and third worlds
and corrupt as if America wasn't

Everyone who speaks my language has bad teeth
and a hand out that wants to be greased

What's the word for *want*
or *want to have?*

as synonym for pay = name
= crime = proof of my desperation

as I enter a dark room
like a latecomer to my own movie

where there's a table with a can of Coke
and a bare bulb that's from the torture scene

they say your mother was an American
Is the crime mother or country?

and I am broken down in front of
the small-boned men and I must insist

in spite of it all I am fit to mother
all this because of the failure

Song of the Little Zion Baptist Church

It takes a mule to get to Tishibee
it takes becoming a mule

with no sense of the Sabbath or depravity
or the judgment or the fire kindled in wrath

It takes the mule's lineage and hard use
and the pull from the trough where woodsmoke

rises since Dixie. On this spot in 1850
a brush arbor built of wood milled in the hollow

and hidden against the master
and a roof put up so they could sing unheard

the planks dragged and mauled and churched up
under the leadership of Burnett Smith

the name of slaveholder and slave, the call
and response. My name in another skin

I nose around in the graveyard
I eat the bindweed and the briar

*   *   *

The light's double exposure, the heat's animal presence
and human complaint, being of two minds

one mind Northern, nostalgic, cold, can't dance
one mind Southern, curried, warm, stirred together

the way the victim is the spleen of the killer
and the killer is the worm of the corpse

On this spot in January, 1996
the church burned to the ground

even his forgiveness singed
the joyful noise, impossible not to hear

then *rebuilt and rededicated to justice*
and god, with grace, love and labor

of Quakers, members, and volunteers
splinters of the burnt church rise

through the new black asphalt
My quiet is their hosanna

Song with Cement

Try to stay out of the way
I was told by my new employer

I lugged bricks for houses of the not-so-rich
I thought I was James Dean

on film, a white ghost in T-shirt who wishes
to be desired for his dumb struggle with

the word or dead in a car crash. That's what I wished
Of my soft hands, of the riots in the city

I would say nothing, but I remember
I got what I didn't deserve: cash from his pocket

tens and twenties from a wad, too much, I pocketed
because how else would I come to speak of my secrets

made out of the crimes I would imagine
burning and looting the cities I made and coming

on her breasts. Two minds of Harlem and Hollywood
Pepper the mud—that was the other command

barked at me. *Plato,* he called me, *Dreamer*
he was guessing and true. *Pepper the mud*

I drew the hoe through the chest of the watery slab
I plotted to betray the white boy with money

*   *   *

Nothing spires. Clouds like the broken lines of the *I Ching*
Heaven and water go their opposite ways

Conflict means not to love. The faces of the N train
awake to the No-Way: the boy looks like the young

James Baldwin who worships at the church of style
and testifies. Style will save us, more than

capital and its engines that take us in one direction
like the lovesick to Long Island City

to Costco and the museum
to the spilled evangelism of sport in the parks

What do you mean you don't dream? You just don't remember
the dream of boxes filled with blood and gauzy things I must unpack

the dream of men whose overcoats open to six pink fetuses
These are my Costco and my museum

One cannot engage in conflict, the oracle says. *One turns*
back and submits to fate. Style is your sentence, your dissatisfied

having. What to wear? The slave shirt and chains, the blue shoes
with three-inch heels of esteem? The Khmer rouge

wears a tennis sweater. The pugilist's in jewels
I remember now: at the museum blocks of basalt and paper

torn from dream, torsos and thin skins
the world's blood has been subtracted from

Song with Spanish Shoes

Self-styled: the pimp roll in porkpie hat, Hi-boy collar and
Dago sweat from emerald bottles. The titillation of pegged pants, self-

fondled bondage, worn to dandy, worn to bliss, so tight we had
to take our socks off first, gartered like a renaissance prince, the *voluptas*

of Spanish shoes ordered through the catalogs in *Ebony* whose names
were cabala of cool, kick and flash, the pleasure came in black and brown

forms of dominate and be, sissy and de Sade, in calf and lizard, in genie
we buffed and rubbed up into sea-deep reflections of ourselves

the retributions of dance, our politics, twitching in the unnamed
face of the atrocious white of the tracts, the hair shirt of lawns

the merciless ice cream faces. We fashioned ourselves
The raw-heeled strut, the pinch of pleasure

from running the gauntlet through, but smoothly
the lower air, the jerky sidewalks, the ruthless selfsame blocks

The rapture of being wrong. Our faces, our necks shaved, girlie
like an armpit or crotch. When nicked, soothed by a styptic pencil

that rabid froth at dad's blue blades. Our hair like Caesar's, tonsured
singe treatment and hot comb, a scalp-scalding part to look other

to be snipped from that manifest, fissureless future of the West
From Philadelphia we saw the Conestoga wagons as white slave ships

By style, by diet of god-liver and onions, we slipped into the shoes
of beauty, or we turned our backs on the serious that chucked us

under the chin. A belt around the package and we were fit
for no school or work, slashed characters in stripes and plaids

we could not be president, not with our tongues laced
with the scars of our tribe

                  *   *   *

       Brought up by de Beauvoir after the war
       I remember a bathtub outdoors with other darlings

       a sitz bath that might have been a quarantine
       or glory—the sun and the warm water sloshing over the lip

       Eisenhower dried us with his stiff white towel
       bristling and stubbled like the beard of the father

       that left our skin compliant. Thus begins the disclosure
       Thus begins the beginning over again and

       the news of what everyone wants. It must be
       the someone else that events happened to

       a murder by the jilted, an uprising, a blush
       We learned tact: the compromise between the unruly

and the absolute. It was a dance in which she led and
she followed, backwards and in heels, a slavish life

of spin and dip. Unfallen
a life of recuperation from not falling

How did we become so
decent? How did the thought creep in

to our creases and ducts and tubes
How did we become so schooled

We let ourselves out of our hands
spilled out of both hands and the body

and into the barracks, the factory
the semi-gloss white houses and the family

We must make a pact
with the sad fat man

Reverse Cowgirl

In this position he's the furloughed sailor
or Whitman under a linden, prone, hands locked

under head, face up, loafing and leaning, observing
a spear of summer grass or stretched out

on the psychiatrist's couch of late humanism
or dead on a bed slab. She's on top but

facing away, having taken him inside
her. She's both him and her for a minute

kneeling—is there anymore cause to kneel
never, never, never, never

unless we're Catholic or the crippled
She looks away, forward, through the window into the rain

reigning in the beast, bridled—that's what *meek* means
she taught him. She taught him the catechism

of umbrage, rage, the rub, being beside oneself
Oh, that's what the love and

be loved was: all inside the instant
inside the old ones: sullen and fractious

inside their knife-worked kitchens and gunplay bedrooms
where there was a rue, an attar

and ambergris of everything they loved for
their gods to be. She looks out the window at the rain

then closes her eyes
then he looks up, mercy come down on him

please, burn a hole through the above

        *   *   *

      A genius, a sadist, a ghosted self
      but before any knot of sex culture race name

      a sound, okay, a noise, a voice
      a little boy crying in his closet

      a bluebottle buzzing in a jar
      just that with a mute in the throat

      like a singer of a missing note that could sob or crack
      it had to be body body

      before it was god in a chord
      that erased the voice or held back or effaced

      goofed, reversed, kicked along, touched
      with the tender and haunting like the bodies of the dead

      feeling more than you can believe
      it was clean and vehemently cool, an attitude

everything improvised, and therefore real
a latent fire which could, but chooses not to

burst into flame
love songs tell you how someone else

makes love . . . The words of love songs
are for people who aren't having sex

when we have no words
we find the cool silences

cool like someone not sweating it
but being, brooding, rude, inarticulate

Strong Female Lead

Something in black and white, studio shot
costumed in crêpe de Chine and bias-cut silk

boxed and bobbed girls, made dreamy, varnished
then unpacked like the steamer trunk of shadows

and smeared them around the room
Enter the woman

in that moment the *question* of who we were
was who we were. The eyes went bad

when the windows broke, but the looking did not stop
the body did not stop. It was the best picture

of the spirit, the psalms and tools we invented
from the partial we filled in with what we were

             *   *   *

        Possessed as if by ghosts of ghosts
        healthy, blooded ghosts not the filmy dead

        weather, the turbulent space we occupied
        and kicked out the vested gods of a decade

and smoked their cigars
in that perfume we clothed ourselves

monstrous American boys in the dark
Then there was what we could see

and what we could feel—the difference
opened until the opening was light

was *mother*—the word recovered from the black
box after the flight went down

Double Portrait

Bruce Smith is a three-headed monster: dog
golden boy, felon. A tarot pack of protection tattoos

warding off devils or land mines. He marries
only to leave for Tahiti again and again

and gets arrested for nudity and spends his francs
on prostitutes and canned goods. *The flesh*

is sad, and I have read all the books, he says
and flees. Bruce Smith is secretly

prepared to betray all that he loves
Bruce Smith loves his luv, loves

that part which is the third rail of the subway
taken in his teeth. It's the sentiment

that's obscene. Bruce Smith is a bad tenor singing
to express his love in an encoded aria

while all the time his fly is down
The demon enters. He has no history but

an ecstasy. He loves what can't be redeemed
without hope. Bruce Smith has an *other* ache

Enough is not enough
The words fail to keep away

the demons. See his stump
his eyes gone, blinded from the explosion

           *   *   *

I was a worker in the sex industry, an actress
concealed when off duty in a work shirt, work boots, overalls

hair up in a baseball hat—contemporary dyke wear
to hide the body from the jones, the cleavage from the clientage

and even from myself. The last thing I want is to go up
or down the stairs each time we munch the sheets and fake

it. My parent's house in Port Arthur, Texas, unveils
the picture within the picture of the child within the child

binding myself and cross dressing and enjoying the pleasure
of being little at the hands of my mother, at the lips of my father

What they said became the part of the body I loved
the ringing, the fluctuating in out, remote near

choked and open voice. I was a secretary at the Securities
Exchange, then a waitress, a dancer, and when I went back

to school, I found this work which is a narrow window
into what it is to be a man—a good suck, three positions

and a cum shot—easy, except for the ones—boys and girls
who want perspective—that way of seeing that makes the world

flat and the illusion real, that's the hard
part, not the erection, when your powers intersect with pleasure

or vice versa, those who can put the mouth on that
that's the man or woman to shun or to marry

Stills

An American girlhood: I served the snacks
in aprons, spit in the oysters. Here's one of me with my father

before he fell off the executive swivel chair and cracked
and clowned, but did not sacrifice like a clown to save me

I'm daddy's little girl at the murky water's edge
These are his knees I'm hugging like sequoias, my face

I'm vamping. Look at those legs. The glasses are drained
At the lake with Popadom, the terrier I was allergic to

my father backed over him in his car. He had to breathe into
a tube to start it. I loved that dog. Spread eagle

with my best friend, Kim, killed in Bosnia. Before
the nose job. Prom. I fell in love with my science teacher

I was lonely. I had lost my mother. Here we are in California
in the end zone, saved in a goofy kind of way

                *   *   *

    Not me, not me, not me, but something enemy
    the blood through the birth chord baby knows is poison

is mother. Rare blood, then the holding, the honey
the rest of her life. Of the two kinds of torture

being held eternally or being held occasionally
the former is suffocation, the later is the big kiss off

There are names and ceremonies for the century
tortures with names like *the telephone, the tea party*

football, the last gasp of pomp at the end of empire
We need more drums and pipes, more glittering things

more artifice, more power. We're foreign to ourselves
body and antibody. What's the ritual for this

the insult of being one of many
one of everything I miss

Song Disowned

Missed the point
the spot on the lungs I thought was the end of a wire

to a telephone ringing in a dream
calling me home. You were in the dream

your black hair using all the light
I thought the mother death was drugstore

loss, numbskull emotional self-help
from glossy magazines spindled in offices

of oncology and MS in social work
When I asked my mother where she was

on the scale of the green to red Pain Chart
that hung on the wall of the office of the Pain Clinic

I thought she'd point me to
amber or buttercup or at worst primrose

but pointed to the scalding red end
So I became the prodigal in green

she became the Dean of Morphine
red queen of our orphancy changing all we knew of dream

into body, and all we knew of body
milked of god and goodbye

*   *   *

    Changed my mind
    left the kitchen and its ragu for the moon

    the Sea of Nectar, the Sea of Fertility. Left the line
    and its fucking clarity for the lake effect

    Clarity, like truth, is Mussolini. I loved
    the uniforms, the horses in harness, trains on time, belief

    in place of reckoning, feeling. Changed my mind about
    drinking the cyanide, shooting the Mexican tar heroin

    into my arm—just a taste—changed arms
    wrapped in surgical tubing like phylacteries, a prayer

    for a vein, for a killed god. Changed wills
    changed number, changed rhythm, changed brain

    from fight and flight to love in the time of contingency
    Changed when I held you, changed saturations, changed hues

    I grew a limb, like a starfish, I grew a wound
    I could not change the despoiling

    world, the deal we had with it to be gorgeous
    damaged, repeated. Changed case and font

changed what I wanted, changed Texas to Paris
changed fear to pear, changed all the menace

into this: I adore you and can't live
without you

How I Came to Believe in the Soul

I was one end of the telephone
my mother, the ex-marine, on the other measuring

the ticks outraged at the cost of the long distance
imagining a patched-through communiqué from Iwo

to Kwajalein to Philadelphia during the war
when the women manned switchboards

which channeled the soul, while I was prodigal
in her estimation, impractical, interior boy

in her estimation, a profligate monk, decadence
of one who did not know the Depression or did not make

the sacrifice: the phone is the fetish of the hidden face
hushed and kissed and told like the sublime

my feeling (coiled and choked back) or the grand enterprise
bandaged as the voices were crossed by radio

where she subdued the Voodoo gods
of mood indigo, of shame and swoon

she had to be the conscience of the body
I inhabited like the zombie

who went after the goddess to the paradise
of fields where I worked (I wanted a car and a vacation

was this too much to ask of a vocation?)
My calling was measureless self and measureless

other, nothing special. Later I learned it was my poverty
that tangled with her economy

and my need to sound the unknowing
I felt in my acquaintance with the world

(I can't say life) my testimony
of untold secrets and the reflexive verbs

of fear about her and for me and fear of being
orphan. Before she hung up she extracted

promises of reflexive visits I resisted
Then I hung up and ended all my apostrophe

Mother Mambo, squeeze every O
of slaves' blood from my veins

                    *   *   *

        I was a Soulist, blinking homunculus with the buzz
        of the molecules making me sentimental, an ESP

        of feeling coming from the memory of still photographs
        of the mushroom cloud and nullifying atoms, seraphs

in the background behind mother/father, downpours
of light obliterating the faces or shadowing faces of the adored

I was a Soulist when I felt something
looking into the Grand Canyon that was maybe looking

itself and not some subcutaneous blush
of the languorous, a dreamy dream like the rush

of the narcotic perfume of the real in musical
or infantile forms. Sheets thrown over the furniture (soulful)

in foreign films (all that sad finale) or sheets over you
ghost or sham Klansman, were many artifacts of you

white, Italian, English, something, the one-quarter
Russian Jew you looked like a Korean boy

in the photos, a boy in his protean
forms of statue or satyr, playing war or baseball

sampling a stance from the young Willie Mays
and so the soul was formed from a ballplayer

who formed his soul in Westfield, Alabama
or in the dust of Puerto Rico, each occasion a drama

of becoming that you later learned was
Michaelangelo or a blow to the solar plexus

greater than the sentiments of calla lilies
My heart sutra said (soulfully)

there must be a fallacy to the pathetic hankering
the ash from the fire in the belly

and your class warfare and your sympathies are spoils
of soul. I pled allegiance to the rainbowed and oily

cloud that floated free of mattering yet mattered to me
I was a Soulist until I found myself smelling the honeysuckle

and loving my cozy place by the beautiful
while carving crosses on the foreheads of the infidels

Song of the Soul as Miles Davis

Come to Paris and be my breath
he sang in the snow of Syracuse. He loved her

(and forgot the war) as she took him to his difficulty
his discredited kisses, his poverty, his pornography

his proletariat wishes
some tuck in, some feet up after work

with hammer and Skil saw, the unsaid paycheck-terror
He's afraid in his heart there's a flaw, a kink, a fissure

a muteness and not something minted
in the mouth. He loved a revisionista

who said all the songs were wrong
the father was raptor; the mother, buzzard

baby became bastard, river became trickle
fat became the soul as thin as a playing card

Of Eros, what can be said that wasn't labor/management
any wonder was ponder, anything dull was deadly

Did he mention that he loved her deeply as the snows and
with that clemency? Because of her he saw something

blink, never mind, it doesn't matter, he shoveled
until spring: sweet was stank, vision transgression, now

he loves her again (what's the war
compared to his agonizing?). Remember

when the personal pronouns were stigmas and styles
little knots where vague is lovely, wandering

from crime to evidence: bed to genitals to afterglow
to *x* to ink. Who will stay after the war

to police the we/they, to launder the I/you
because of her he saw something

blink—one figure, one small heart yes
but powerless against her and the world

              *   *   *

        Before the burden of the cool
        and the haute couture silk robes from Japan

        before you were a black man making seven figures
        You asked what's music for?

        Exhaustion and downbeat
        you always wanted to be kicked loose

        of the resistances and stroke
        of the new so everything begins

with *and, and, and,* everything fettered
with association, grafted to the past: elder to exile

to alchemist to Heraclitus to agent provocateur
of death. Moving backwards to soul man to so what

though after all the blackness
the hero is the obstacle of the song

and the song unmakes what made it
You tried on the beautiful suits of jelly bean

and popcorn pimp, your mother's other
you wanted an art with a Ferrari and smack

you wanted an art with lapels narrowing
into a small town on the river where you were

a boy of the late 40s, a blue mood
that reduced all the chords to one, you

wanted no chords or all: you moved
to a barn yard in the Midwest

to vamp and just one last thing
then another . . . You faced away

you wanted to be all selfless music before
it became art and local as a motherfucker